Prayer
JOURNAL

This Book Belongs To:

_____

_____

Simply Blessed

Thank you for your purchase!

If you are happy with this prayer journal, we would love to hear about it. Please leave a review. Honest reviews help customers find the right book for their needs and also helps us create better books.

Meaningful Bible Verses

Stressed...........................Matthew 11:25-30

Worried..............................Matthew 8:18-31

Upset......................................John 14

Scared..............................Joshua 1:1-9

Lonely.....................................Psalm 23

Anxious.........................Philippians 4:4-9

Sick..Psalm 41

Unhappy........................Colossians 3:12-17

Depressed..............................Psalm 27

Losing hope.............................Psalm 139

Sinned....................................Psalm 51

Hurt.......................................John 15

Weak...............................Psalm 18:1-29

In danger.................................Psalm 91

Lack of faith.............................Exodus 14

Date: _____

Verse of the day:

Reflect on What God is calling you to do in this passage?

Questions I have?

I praise God for...

Date: _____

Love Like Jesus

I'm thankful for...

I'm sorry for...

I'd like to pray for...

Date: _____

Favorite Bible Verses

JESUS
is ♥

Favorite Prayer

Faith can move Mountains

Date: _____

Verse of the day:

Reflect on What God is calling you to do in this passage?

Questions I have?

I praise God for...

Date: _____

Love Like Jesus

I'm thankful for...

I'm sorry for...

I'd like to pray for...

Favorite Bible Verses

JESUS *is* →♥

Date: _____

Favorite Prayer

Faith can move Mountains

Date: _____

Verse of the day:

Reflect on What God is calling you to do in this passage?

Questions I have?

I praise God for...

Date: _____

Love Like Jesus

I'm thankful for...

I'm sorry for...

I'd like to pray for...

Date: _____

Favorite Bible Verses

JESUS
≫≫ is →
♥

Favorite Prayer

Faith can move Mountains

Date: _____

Verse of the day:

Reflect on What God is calling you to do in this passage?

Questions I have?

I praise God for...

Date: _____

Love Like Jesus

I'm thankful for...

I'm sorry for...

I'd like to pray for...

Date: _____

Favorite Bible Verses

JESUS
is ♥

Date: _____

Favorite Prayer

Faith can move Mountains

Date: _____

Verse of the day:

Reflect on what God is calling you to do in this passage?

Questions I have?

Date: _____

I praise God for...

Love Like Jesus

I'm thankful for...

I'm sorry for...

I'd like to pray for...

Date: _____

Favorite Bible Verses

JESUS
is ➤
♥

Date: _____

Favorite Prayer

Faith
can move
Mountains

Verse of the day:

Reflect on What God is calling you to do in this passage?

Questions I have?

I praise God for...

Date: _____

Love Like Jesus

I'm thankful for...

I'm sorry for...

I'd like to pray for...

Favorite Bible Verses

JESUS
is →
♥

Favorite Prayer

Faith can move Mountains

Date: _____

Verse of the day:

Reflect on What God is calling you to do in this passage?

Questions I have?

I praise God for...

Date: _____

Love Like Jesus

I'm thankful for...

I'm sorry for...

I'd like to pray for...

Favorite Bible Verses

JESUS
»» is →
♥

Favorite Prayer

Faith can move Mountains

For God

so loved  the world,

that he gave his

only begotten Son,

that whosoever

BELIEVETH IN HIM

should not perish,

but have

EVERLASTING

LIFE.

John 3:16 KJV

Date: _____

Verse of the day:

Reflect on What God is calling you to do in this passage?

Questions I have?

I praise God for...

Date: _____

Love *Like* Jesus

I'm thankful for...

I'm sorry for...

I'd like to pray for...

Date: _____

Favorite Bible Verses

JESUS
>>> is →
♥

Date: _____

Favorite Prayer

Faith can move Mountains

Verse of the day:

_____

Reflect on What God is calling you to do in this passage?

_____

Questions I have?

I praise God for...

Date: _____

Love Like Jesus

I'm thankful for...

I'm sorry for...

I'd like to pray for...

Favorite Bible Verses

JESUS
is →

Favorite Prayer

Faith can move Mountains

Be a light for all to see

Matthew 5:16

Verse of the day:

Reflect on what God is calling you to do in this passage?

Questions I have?

I praise God for...

Date: _____

Love Like Jesus

I'm thankful for...

I'm sorry for...

I'd like to pray for...

Date: _____

Favorite Bible Verses

JESUS
is ♥

Date: _____

Favorite Prayer

Faith can move Mountains

LEAVE THE *judging* TO JESUS

Date: _____

Verse of the day:

Reflect on What God is calling you to do in this passage?

Questions I have?

I praise God for...

Date: _____

Love Like Jesus

I'm thankful for...

I'm sorry for...

I'd like to pray for...

Date: _____

Favorite Bible Verses

Favorite Prayer

Faith can move Mountains

GRACE

hope

FAITH

JOY

BLESSINGS

Date: _____

Verse of the day:

Reflect on What God is calling you to do in this passage?

Questions I have?

I praise God for...

Date: _____

Love Like Jesus

I'm thankful for...

I'm sorry for...

I'd like to pray for...

Date: _____

Favorite Bible Verses

JESUS *is* ♥

Favorite Prayer

Faith can move Mountains

Faith

OVER →

Fears

Date: _____

Verse of the day:

Reflect on What God is calling you to do in this passage?

Questions I have?

I praise God for...

Date: _____

Love Like Jesus

I'm thankful for...

I'm sorry for...

I'd like to pray for...

Date: _____

Favorite Bible Verses

JESUS
is

Favorite Prayer

Faith can move Mountains

EXERCISE
DAILY
walk with
JESUS
· ·

Date: _____

Verse of the day:

Reflect on What God is calling you to do in this passage?

Questions I have?

I praise God for...

Date: _____

Love Like Jesus

I'm thankful for...

I'm sorry for...

I'd like to pray for...

Favorite Bible Verses

JESUS
is →

Favorite Prayer

Faith *can move* Mountains

Date: _____

Verse of the day:

Reflect on What God is calling you to do in this passage?

Questions I have?

I praise God for...

Date: _____

Love Like Jesus

I'm thankful for...

I'm sorry for...

I'd like to pray for...

Date: _____

Favorite Bible Verses

JESUS
»»»is→
♥

Favorite Prayer

Faith
can move
Mountains

faith

FAMILY

Love

Date: _____

Verse of the day:

Reflect on What God is calling you to do in this passage?

Questions I have?

I praise God for...

Date: _____

Love Like Jesus

I'm thankful for...

I'm sorry for...

I'd like to pray for...

Date: _____

Favorite Bible Verses

JESUS
is ♥

Favorite Prayer

Faith can move Mountains

Date: _____

Verse of the day:

Reflect on What God is calling you to do in this passage?

Questions I have?

I praise God for...

Date: _____

Love
Like
Jesus

I'm thankful for...

I'm sorry for...

I'd like to pray for...

Date: _____

Favorite Bible Verses

JESUS
»»»is→
♥

Date: _____

Favorite Prayer

Faith can move Mountains

Date: _____

Verse of the day:

Reflect on What God is calling you to do in this passage?

Questions I have?

I praise God for...

Date: _____

Love Like Jesus

I'm thankful for...

I'm sorry for...

I'd like to pray for...

Favorite Bible Verses

JESUS
is ❤

Date: _____

Favorite Prayer

Faith can move Mountains

I am the Resurrection and the Life

John 11:25

Verse of the day:

Reflect on What God is calling you to do in this passage?

Questions I have?

I praise God for...

Date: _____

Love Like Jesus

I'm thankful for...

I'm sorry for...

I'd like to pray for...

Date: _____

Favorite Bible Verses

JESUS
≫≫ *is* →
♥

Date: _____

Favorite Prayer

Faith can move Mountains

H IN THIS House we love jesus

Bookmarks

Psalm 67:3-4

HOW beautiful are the FEET of these who PREACH THE GOOD NEWS

Romans 10:15

LET THE NATIONS BE GLAD

GO AND MAKE TICKET 1468 DISCIPLES of ALL NATIONS

Matthew 28:16-20

Important Notes

Made in the USA
Middletown, DE
04 September 2023

37989425R00057